INVESTIGATING
ECOSYSTEMS

SUPER COOL SCIENCE EXPERIMENTS

CHERRY LAKE PRESS
Ann Arbor, Michigan

SCIENCE · INVESTIGATION

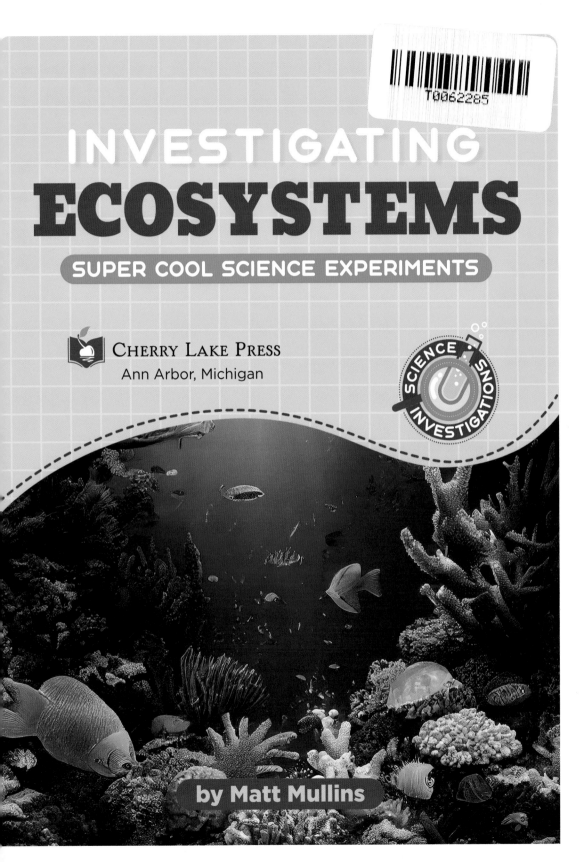

by Matt Mullins

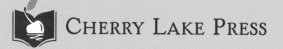 CHERRY LAKE PRESS

Published in the United States of America by
Cherry Lake Publishing Group
Ann Arbor, Michigan
www.cherrylakepublishing.com

Reading Adviser: Beth Walker Gambro, MS, Ed., Reading Consultant, Yorkville, IL

Content Editor: Robert Wolffe, EdD,
Professor of Teacher Education, Bradley University, Peoria, Illinois

Book Designer: Ed Morgan of Bowerbird Books

Grateful acknowledgment to Deborah Simon, Department of Chemistry,
Whitman College

Photo Credits: cover and title page, 4, 6, 7, 8, 16, 19, 23, 24, 29, freepik.com; 5, 9, 11, 13, 15, 17, 18, 21, 22, 25, 27, 28, The Design Lab.

Cherry Lake Press is an imprint of Cherry Lake Publishing Group.

Library of Congress Cataloging-in-Publication Data has been filed and is available at catalog.loc.gov

Printed in the United States of America
Corporate Graphics

A Note to Parents and Teachers: Please review the instructions for these experiments before your children do them. Be sure to help them with any experiments you do not think they can safely conduct on their own.

A Note to Kids: Be sure to ask an adult for help with these experiments when you need it. Always put your safety first!

Note from Publisher: Websites change regularly, and their future contents are outside of our control. Supervise children when conducting any recommended online searches for extended learning opportunities.

CONTENTS

Nature's
COMMUNITIES

When you look at a forest or pond, what comes to mind? You might think about a variety of plants growing next to each other. What about animals? Consider the many kinds of insects, birds, reptiles, and mammals, for example, living in each place. Did you know that animals and plants live together in **ecosystems**? And you can learn about ecosystems through experiments! In this book, we'll carry out experiments using materials you have at home. It's easier than you imagine.

Getting
STARTED

So, what exactly is an ecosystem? It's a network or community of living things and their environments. Scientists learn about ecosystems by carefully studying them. For instance, scientists watch how animals live in their homes, the plants that grow there, and how much water or other resources are there. They discover which plants grow best in different regions. They also examine how plants and animals from one ecosystem move into another.

Scientists then write down their **observations**. They take notes on everything they discover. Sometimes those observations lead to new questions. With new questions in mind, scientists design experiments to find answers!

When scientists design experiments, they often use the scientific method. What is the scientific method? It's a step-by-step process to answer specific questions. The steps don't always follow the same pattern. However, the scientific method often works like this:

STEP ONE: A scientist gathers the facts and makes observations about one particular thing.

STEP TWO: The scientist comes up with a question that is not answered by observations and facts.

STEP THREE: The scientist creates a **hypothesis**. This is a statement about what the scientist thinks might be the answer to the question.

STEP FOUR: The scientist tests the hypothesis by designing an experiment to see whether the hypothesis is correct. Then the scientist carries out the experiment and writes down what happens.

STEP FIVE: The scientist draws a **conclusion** based on the result of the experiment. The conclusion might be that the hypothesis is correct. Sometimes, though, the hypothesis is not correct. In that case, the scientist might develop a new hypothesis and another experiment.

In the following experiments, we'll see the scientific method in action. We'll gather some facts and observations about ecosystems and the life that thrives in them. For each experiment, we'll develop a question and a hypothesis. Next, we'll do an actual experiment to see if our hypothesis is correct. By the end of the experiment, we should know something new about ecosystems. Young scientists, are you ready? Let's get started!

Ecotones

An ecological system is made up of an area and everything that's found in it—plants, animals, rocks, soil, air, and water. It's a community. Some of the life in this community is so tiny that you need a microscope to see it. There are forest ecosystems, ocean ecosystems, and many others.

One of the hardest things about studying an ecosystem is figuring out where one ecosystem ends and the next begins. The place where one ecosystem runs into another is called an **ecotone**. Ecotones have plants and animals from each ecosystem that borders them. Could this mean that more types of wildlife live in an ecotone than the ecosystems that form it? Let's find out. Here is one hypothesis you might want to test: **Ecotones have more plants and animals than the ecosystems right next to them.**

Here's what you'll need:

- An ecotone, where two ecosystems meet
- A big ring (a hula hoop works great)
- A notebook
- A pencil

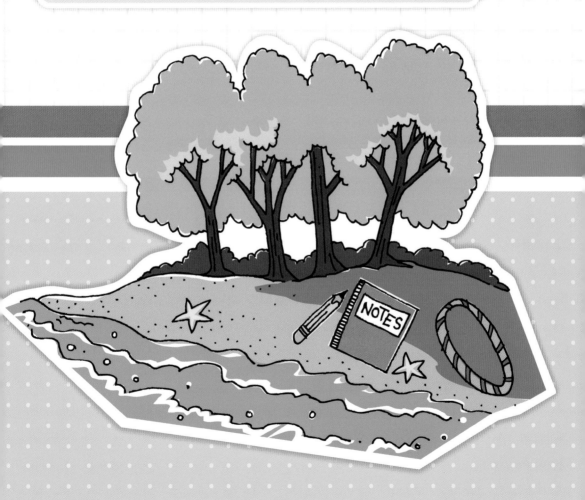

• INSTRUCTIONS •

1. Find an ecotone near you. It can be a forest and a field, a pond and a grassland, or a prairie and a beach. Ask an adult to go with you. Go to the border of the ecosystems. Walk 15 steps into one of the ecosystems. Stop. Toss the ring.

2. Study what you see inside the ring. In your notebook, label one sheet "Ecosystem 1, toss 1." Count how many different types of plants and animals you see. Count trees if they are overhead. Include birds that fly overhead and insects found in the soil. Record the living things that you see and how many of them there are.

3. Now toss the ring nearby. Record the number of different plants and animals you see on a new page, labeled "Ecosystem 1, toss 2."

4. Return to the ecotone. Now walk 15 steps into the other ecosystem. Toss the ring down and record your findings on a sheet labeled "Ecosystem 2, toss 1." Now toss the ring nearby and record your new results on a sheet labeled "Ecosystem 2, toss 2."

5. Go back to the ecotone and toss the ring down there. Record the number of different plants and animals you find on a sheet labeled "Ecotone, toss 1." Repeat the process nearby and write down the results on a sheet labeled "Ecotone, toss 2."

6. Analyze your data. Find the average number of different plants and animals in Ecosystem 1 by adding the two values you recorded and dividing by 2. Round your answer to the nearest whole number. Do the same for Ecosystem 2 and the ecotone.

What can you conclude from this experiment? On average, did you find more kinds of plants, animals, and insects in Ecosystem 1, or the ecotone? Did you see plants and animals from both ecosystems in the ecotone? Is the hypothesis correct or not?

FACTS!

A food chain shows how living things depend on each other for food. The first link in a food chain is a plant. Many animals rely on plants for food. Other animals eat animals. A food web is like a food chain but larger. Food webs show the many ways that living things are connected in order to survive.

EXPERIMENT 2

The Perfect Temperature

Airflow, water supply, and temperature are among the most important factors in a healthy ecosystem. Why do some living things prefer one ecosystem over another? One way we can investigate is by studying yeast, a living thing common to many ecosystems. Yeast emits **carbon dioxide** gas when it feeds. People also use yeast in their kitchens. The gas from yeast creates bubbles in bread as it rises. Yeast, like other living things, requires just the right temperature to survive and thrive. Has your family ever baked a loaf of bread? Recipes often suggest dissolving the yeast in warm water. Why not hot or cold water? Here are three possible hypotheses to choose from:

Hypothesis #1: Yeast works best at lukewarm temperatures.

Hypothesis #2: Yeast works best at cold temperatures.

Hypothesis #3: Yeast works best at hot temperatures.

Here's what you'll need:

- 4 empty 12-ounce (354.9 milliliter) bottles
- A marker
- 4 tablespoons of sugar
- 4 tablespoons of baking yeast (active dry yeast)
- 4 cups
- A 1/2 cup measuring cup
- Ice cubes
- Thermometer
- A microwaveable cup
- Microwave oven
- 4 balloons
- 4 rubber bands
- String
- Ruler
- A notebook

· INSTRUCTIONS ·

1. Label the 4 bottles "A," "B," "C," and "D" with a marker. Place 1 tablespoon of sugar and 1 tablespoon of yeast in each bottle.

2. Label the 4 cups "A," "B," "C," and "D." Measure 1/2 cup of cool water and pour it into Cup A. Then add 1 ice cube.

3. Run warm tap water and check it with a thermometer until it reaches 70°F (21.1°C). Measure 1/2 cup of the warm water and pour it into Cup B.

4. Run the tap water to 100°F (37.8°C). Measure 1/4 cup of the hot water and pour that into Cup C.

5. Pour 1/2 cup of water into a microwavable cup. Place it in the microwave and heat it for 30 seconds. Have an adult help you check the temperature until the water reaches 150°F (65.6°C). Carefully pour the hot water into Cup D.

6. Record the temperatures of each cup in your notebook.

7. Pour the contents of Cup A into Bottle A. Swirl the bottle to mix the yeast, sugar, and water.

8. Stretch the open end of a balloon over the mouth of the bottle. Wrap a rubber band around the area where the balloon covers the bottle to make a tight seal.

9. Do the same with Cup B and Bottle B, Cup C and Bottle C, and Cup D and Bottle D. Work at a quick but safe pace.

10. Now measure the gas produced by the active yeast. Use a string and wrap it around the widest part of the balloon. Remove the string, and use a ruler to measure the length it took to reach around the balloon. Do this every 10 minutes for the next 30 minutes. Record these measurements.

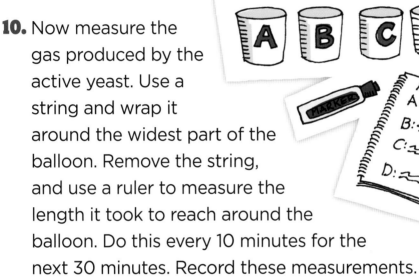

CONCLUSION

Which balloon expanded fastest? Which balloon expanded the least? Which expanded the most? The yeast that produced the most gas was the most active at the temperature of its environment. This yeast inflated the balloon the most. So which temperature was best for the yeast? Yeast needs a little warmth, but water that is too hot or too cold can kill it. Does that fact help explain your results? Was your hypothesis correct?

Diversity Is Good!

In an ecosystem where there is yeast, there are other living things, too. In a healthy, **diverse** ecosystem, plants and animals often help each other. Plants, for example, convert sunlight and rainfall into oxygen. Animals can then use that oxygen.

Sometimes plants release gases that help other nearby plants. Apples and green bananas release a gas called **ethylene**. Ethylene helps certain fruits ripen faster. Some fruits emit more ethylene than others. With that in mind, think about a hypothesis. One possibility you might want to test is: **An apple works better than a banana at helping nearby bananas ripen faster.**

Here's what you'll need:

- 3 small brown paper bags
- A marker
- 1 soft, ripe apple
- 4 green, unripe bananas
- 1 soft, ripe banana
- A notebook

· INSTRUCTIONS ·

1. Label the paper bags "A," "B," and "C" with the marker.

2. Place the apple and 1 unripe banana in Bag A. Place the ripe banana and 1 unripe banana in Bag B. Place 2 unripe bananas in Bag C. Fold down the tops of the bags.

3. Move the bags to 3 locations around your home or school. The locations should have similar temperatures and receive the same amount of light.

4. Wait 2 days and check the bags. In your notebook, write down how ripe the previously green bananas appear. Fold the bags closed again.

5. In 3 days, rate the bananas again. Write down your observations.

6. Wait 3 more days and rate the bananas a final time. Record your observations.

·CONCLUSION·

Which unripe banana ripened fastest? Which ripened slowest? How well did the ripe apple, the ripe banana, and the unripe banana help the other bananas become more ripe? Did your observations lead you to conclude that the apple helped the banana ripen faster than another banana did? Though bananas and apples may not necessarily grow in the same ecosystem in nature, this experiment helps demonstrate how plants can affect each other. Diversity in an ecosystem often helps all living things thrive.

EXPERIMENT 4

Preventing Erosion

Have you ever noticed any worn-down paths at the park? People using the paths probably played a part in wearing them down. Also, rain and wind can cause **erosion** by moving topsoil away. What's left behind often isn't very good for growing new plants.

Plants and soil need one another to stay in place. A healthy ecosystem resists erosion by keeping a good balance of plants and soil together. Let's see if we can explore this relationship with a simple experiment. Think about using plants that you might easily find. How about grass? Now think of a hypothesis that relates to grass and erosion. Here is one option: **Grass reduces erosion.**

Here's what you'll need:

- 2 rectangular baking pans of the same size
- Soil
- Grass seed
- Water
- A thick book
- A pitcher for water

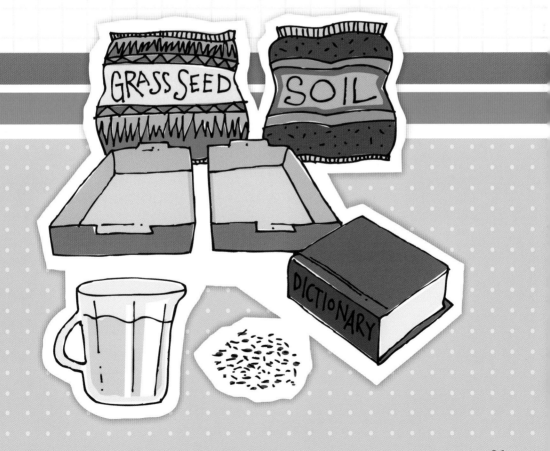

· INSTRUCTIONS ·

1. Fill each baking pan with soil.

2. In one pan, sprinkle grass seeds on the surface and press them into the soil.

3. In the other pan, press the soil, but don't add seeds.

4. Water each pan thoroughly and place them in a window where they can get sunlight.

5. Wait for the grass to sprout. This step might take 7 days or longer.

6. Once the grass is a few inches tall, place the book flat on your work surface. Now place one end of each pan on the edge of the book.

7. This part of the experiment could get messy, so be sure you are working in an area that can be easily cleaned. Fill a pitcher with water. Pour the water into the pans from the top, one pan at a time.

·CONCLUSION·

How does the water affect the soil in both pans? Does the water move a lot of the soil? What about the grassy soil? What does this tell you about how plants affect soil erosion? Is your hypothesis correct?

FACTS!

By 2023, the world had lost about one-third of its forests. That amount is equal to an area twice the size of the United States. Most of this loss is due to human activity, including logging and clearing land for farming and housing. How might these activities cause serious soil erosion? What impact do you think this has on the animals and plants in a forest ecosystem?

EXPERIMENT 5

Pollution and Plant Growth

Soil is an important part of many ecosystems. Plants add **nutrients** to the soil when they die and rot. Animals spread seeds and nutrients when they eat and make waste. In a healthy ecosystem, plants and animals keep adding nutrients to the soil.

However, humans often pollute the air, water, and soil. For example, cars release harmful gases and some can leak oil. The **pesticides** we use kill beneficial insects and can poison the environment. Pollution makes it difficult for ecosystems to support plants and animals, clean and filter water, and make oxygen for many living things to breathe. Do you think pollution can make it difficult for seeds to grow? That question is the focus of our next experiment. Come up with your own hypothesis or try testing this one:
A small amount of pollution prevents seeds from growing as well as they could without pollution.

Here's what you'll need:

- Paper towels (1 or 2 sheets)
- 3 jar lids
- A marker
- 3 resealable plastic bags
- 3 medicine droppers
- 30 radish seeds
- A notebook
- Motor oil
- A teaspoon
- Laundry detergent
- A 1/4 cup measuring cup
- Water
- Aluminum foil
- Ruler

· INSTRUCTIONS ·

1. Cut the paper towels into a circular shape to fit inside the jar lids. Place one circle in each lid.

2. Using a marker, label each lid "A," "B," and "C." Label each plastic bag "A," "B," and "C."

3. Fill 1 medicine dropper with water. Drip water onto the paper towel in Lid A, counting the drops until the towel is fully damp. Write down the number of drops in your notebook. Place 10 radish seeds on the paper towel. Set this lid on Bag A.

4. Fill another dropper with motor oil. Ask an adult to help you. Drip the same number of drops you used with Lid A onto the paper towel in Lid B. Place 10 radish seeds in Lid B, spaced as before. Set this lid on Bag B.

5. Mix 1/2 teaspoon laundry detergent with 1/4 cup water. Fill the third dropper with the detergent water. Drip the detergent water onto the towel in Lid C. Use the same number of drops that you used for Lids A and B. Place 10 radish seeds in Lid C. Set Lid C on Bag C.

6. Carefully wrap each lid with foil. Place each wrapped lid in its labeled bag and seal the bags. Set the sealed jar lids aside.

7. After 5 days, remove each lid from the bag and unwrap them. Many of the seeds will have shoots.

8. Count the seeds with shoots and record the number for each lid in your notebook. Measure the length of the shoots and record this data for each lid.

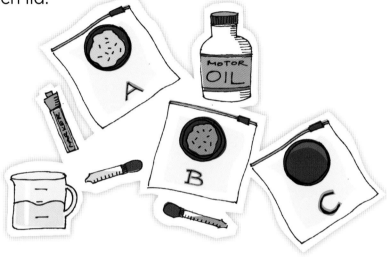

·CONCLUSION·

In which lid did the seeds produce the most shoots? In which lid were the shoots the longest? In which were there the fewest sprouted seeds? How would you explain the seed behavior in each sample? The detergent mixture represents the chemicals and soapsuds that might pollute the environment from washing a car. Can you guess why we used motor oil? What do your results tell you about the impact of pollution on plants and ecosystems?

· EXPERIMENT 6 ·

Do It Yourself!

We've learned many things from our experiments and observations of ecosystems. So where do you go from here? You may know from science class that plants turn sunlight into oxygen. Did you know that this is true even in underwater ecosystems? Can you create an experiment to examine how important sunlight is to a water ecosystem? What is a possible hypothesis? You might want to test this one: **Even under water, green plants need sunlight.** What kind of mini-ecosystem could you create to test this hypothesis? Experiment and see what happens!

FACTS!

Studying ecosystems can take you all over the world—from tropical rain forests, deserts, and mountain meadows to the deepest depths of the ocean and even your own backyard. Exploring ecosystems is a great science adventure!

Glossary

carbon dioxide (KAR-buhn dye-OK-side) a gas that is a mixture of carbon and oxygen

conclusion (kuhn-KLOO-zhuhn) a final decision, thought, or opinion

diverse (dih-VURSS) varied

ecosystems (EE-koh-siss-tuhmz) communities of plants and animals interacting with their environment

ecotone (EE-kuh-tohn) an area between two ecological communities

erosion (ih-ROH-zuhn) the process by which the surface of the earth is worn away by water or wind, for example

ethylene (ETH-uh-leen) a gas that speeds the ripening of fruits

hypothesis (hye-POTH-uh-sihss) a logical guess about what will happen in an experiment

nutrients (NOO-tree-uhntss) things that are needed by plants, animals, and humans to stay healthy

observations (ob-zur-VAY-shuhnz) things that are seen or noticed with one's senses

pesticides (PESS-tuh-sidz) chemicals used to kill insects and other pests

For More Information

BOOKS

Ignotofsky, Rachel. *The Wondrous Workings of Planet Earth: Understanding Our World and Its Ecosystems*. Berkeley, CA: Ten Speed Press, 2018.

Latham, Donna. *Biomes: Discover the Earth's Ecosystems with Environmental Science Activities for Kids*. Norwich, VT: Nomad Press, 2019.

Woodward, John. *Habitats of the World*. New York: DK Publishing, 2023.

WEBSITES
Explore these online sources with an adult:

Britannica Kids: Ecosystems

NASA: 10 Interesting Things About Ecosystems

PBS Kids: Jungle Jeopardy—An Ecosystem Game

Index

About the Author

Matt Mullins holds a master's degree in the history of science. Matt writes about science and technology, and sometimes about food, culture, and other things that interest him. He lives in Madison, Wisconsin, with his wife and son.